Darwin ○

Alice Springs ○ ○**Ltyentye Apurte Community**

T0362825

1

Ltyentye Apurte is in the Northern Territory. You say it like *L-ginger Porter*. Can you try and say it? It means a clump of beefwood trees. These trees can be seen all along the roads and hills. You can find our town 80 kilometres along a dirt road from **Mparntwe** (M-barn-twa) - Alice Springs. It is also known in English as **Santa Teresa**.

Knowledge Books and Software

3

Ltyentye Apurte has a population of around 555 people. Most of them are **Eastern Arrernte** (arr-run-da). The main language spoken is Eastern Arrernte. Some people also speak other Aboriginal languages. English is our community's second or third language for most people. Eastern Arrernte is also taught at our school. Can you speak a second language?

Knowledge Books and Software

5

There are four main sacred sites in Santa Teresa. It is important for us to learn about our **apmere** (ab-mar-a) - our country. These sites tell us stories about:

· Ltyentye Apurte - beefwood tree

· **Atyenhenge Atherre** (at-ch-eng-a-the-rra) - grandfather and grandson

· **Keringke** (ka-ring-ka) - kangaroo foot

· **mpwerlarre** (m-b-le-rra) - rainbow hill.

These stories are very important to know and pass down.

Knowledge Books and Software

7

Ltyentye Apurte is red, yellow, and sandy. It has lots of rocks and rolling, big hills. Visitors should always ask the Ltyentye Apurte peoples before climbing any of these hills. They are sacred. This means that they are special to our community and important to our culture. Do you have any sacred sites in your town?

Knowledge Books and Software

When you drive into Ltyentye Apurte, you can see Santa Teresa Church. Our Church was built in 1953 by the local people and the missionaries. The missionaries were sent to our town by the catholic church. Our church was painted by local Elders in many beautiful colours. The paintings share the spiritual stories and beliefs of our community.

10

There are 3 suburbs in Ltyentye Apurte: Old Village, New House, and East Side. The houses here are bright colours of red, green, blue, and yellow. There is one old stone house left. These were built by the men back when the mission people came. Most peoples moved here from a place called **Arltungke** (arl-tung-ka).

Knowledge Books and Software

13

We have an indoor basketball court and a skate ramp at our rec hall. We play there and do fun activities after school. In the holidays, there are big barbecues and discos. The children from our community painted the rec hall mural in bright colours. What colours can you see? There is also a community swimming pool that opens in the hot season, in October. There are so many fun things to do in our town!

Knowledge Books and Software

Knowledge Books and Software

Philipson Bore is 8km from our community. Our main water supply comes from here. There are many kinds of horses at the bore. Students at our school get to do horse riding lessons. There is a picnic and camping ground at the bore. Visitors can ask for permission to come and camp. It is a calm place to have a yarn around the fire and cook some **aherre** (a-ha-rra) - kangaroo tail. If we are lucky, after big rain we can swim in the bore tank!

16

You can find many animals in Ltyentye Apurte like:

- **perentie** (per-en-tee) - lizards
- **irrarnte** (irr-an-da) - black cockatoos
- **angepe** (a-nga-pa) - crows
- **nanthe** (nun-tha) - horses
- **apmwe** (ub-mwa) - king brown snakes
- **mpwaltye** (m-b-wal-tch-a) - frogs.

The frogs hide deep down in the dam and come up after big rain. The snakes come out in the hot season. They hide in the **aywerte** (ay-oor-ta) - spinifex.

18

We have a local garden in Ltyentye Apurte. Many different things are grown here like kale, chilli, spinach, and mulberries. We also have lots of herbs and native flowers. We learn how to grow things that will handle our climate. This is hard because our climate is very hot and dry. It is important to know how to work with the land you live on and care for it.

Knowledge Books and Software

We have an art centre called **Keringke** (ka-ring-ka) Arts where the local men and women make art. Keringke means kangaroo foot. The women paint in bright colours. The men make:

- shields called **alkwerte** (al-kur-da)

- spears called **irrtyarte** (ir-char-ta)

- boomerangs called **alye** (a-le-ya).

The men use ironbark tree wood to make them. Many people from all over the world come to visit Keringke Arts. They come to learn about the traditional work of our oldest living culture. We hope you can come and visit us one day too! **Kele** (ku-la).

Knowledge Books and Software

23

Word bank

Ltyentye Apurte (L-ginger-Porter) catholic

Territory beautiful

beefwood spiritual

population basketball

Eastern Arrernte (arr-run-da) activities

aboriginal barbecues

languages Philipson Bore

community permission

sacred traditional

important

Keringke (ka-ring-ka)

kangaroo foot

missionaries

Knowledge Books and Software